T0012437

TERROR STRIKES NEW YORK

ON SEPTEMBER 11

A HISTORY-SEEKING ADVENTURE

by Thomas Kingsley Troupe

CAPSTONE PRESS
a capstone imprint

Published by You Choose, an imprint of Capstone
1710 Roe Crest Drive, North Mankato, Minnesota 56003
capstonepub.com

Library of Congress Cataloging-in-Publication Data is available on the Library of
Congress website.

ISBN 9781669069478 (library binding)
ISBN 9781669069447 (paperback)
ISBN 9781669069454 (ebook PDF)

Summary: YOU are in New York City on a sunny September morning when
suddenly a huge passenger plane flies straight into one tower of the World Trade
Center. A short time later, a second plane slams into the other tower. Clouds of
black smoke billow from the towers. Will you rush into the buildings and try to
help any survivors? Or will you try to escape the burning wreckage falling to the
street? Step back in time to face the dangers and difficult decisions real people had
to face on one of America's darkest days.

Editorial Credits
Editor: Aaron Sautter; Designer: Bobbie Nuytten; Media Researcher: Jo Miller;
Production Specialist: Whitney Schaefer

Image Credits
Alamy: American Photo Archive, 39, dpa picture alliance, 69, Ivo Roospold, 87;
Associated Press: picture-alliance/dpa/Hubert Boesl, Cover; Getty Images: Alex
Wong, 106, Andrew Lichtenstein, 34, Carmen Taylor, 81, Ezra Shaw, 46, Hiro
Oshima, 79, Mario Tama, 97, Matt Moyer, 37, 95, Spencer Platt, 23, Thomas
Nilsson, 66; Newscom: ZUMAPRESS/Harald Franzen, 18; Shutterstock:
Anakins srk, 57, Anthony Correia, 74, dcwcreations, 49, Reuber Duarte, 104,
Robert R French, 4, Ryan DeBerardinis, 8, serhii.suravikin, 98

Printed and bound in China. PO 5827

TABLE OF CONTENTS

ABOUT YOUR JOURNEY

September 11, 2001, began as a typical sunny day in New York City. But that morning, life in the United States changed forever. The air was soon filled with the sounds of roaring jet plane engines, deafening explosions, and the terrified screams of thousands of people.

When terrorists attacked the World Trade Center in New York, it destroyed the lives of thousands of people. How will you respond when you find yourself in the middle of the chaos on that day? Follow the directions at the bottom of the pages. Your choices will determine your fate. When you finish one path, go back and read the others for new perspectives of what people experienced on that dreadful day.

Turn the page to begin your journey.

CHAPTER 1

LIFE IN THE BIG CITY

It's a beautiful morning in New York City. The sun is out, and the sky is blue. It's another typical busy day in the Big Apple. Traffic is moving through the streets. Taxis are dropping people off for their workday. The sidewalks are crowded with everyone moving to their destinations.

In Manhattan, a fire fighting crew is heading back to its station. The crew had answered a fire alarm call at a pastry shop. But there were no signs of fire or smoke. So, a firefighter checked and reset the malfunctioning alarm. Then the crew hopped back into the truck to return to the station.

Turn the page.

The fire truck soon passes a pair of tourists standing on a sidewalk by their hotel. They look up at the buildings in awe. They're amazed by the busy streets of New York City.

One of them steps to the curb to hail a taxicab. Three taxis pass by before one slows to a stop. The tourists high-five each other and then climb into the backseat. They tell the driver to take them to a well-known breakfast spot named Gregory's.

Across the street, a businessperson in an expensive suit stops at their favorite coffee stand. As they wait for their order, they check out their hair in the reflection of a nearby building's windows. The new haircut is short, but they seem satisfied. They're just not sure how their coworkers in the World Trade Center will react. They take their cup of coffee, slide a cardboard sleeve around it, and head off to their workday.

These three people are just a few among thousands who will experience the worst day in New York City's history.

To witness the disaster as a tourist, turn to page 11.
To be a World Trade Center employee, turn to page 41.
To work as a New York City firefighter, turn to page 71.

CHAPTER 2

TERROR IN THE SKY

You've never been to New York City before. But you and your brother Reid wanted to explore the world's greatest city. Having grown up on a farm in the Midwest, downtown New York is a completely different experience for you. There are people everywhere. And tall skyscrapers stretch as far as you can see. You spent your first day at Central Park. Reid wanted to go to the zoo there. You weren't too excited about it. There are plenty of animals on the farm, after all.

Turn the page.

"How often do you get to see animals in the middle of a giant city?" Reid asked.

"Okay," you replied. "But after that, we're doing something less stinky."

Today you got to decide where to go. You got up early and headed to the southern part of Manhattan. You heard there was a great place there to get breakfast.

Your cab driver lets you off at the corner of Rector and Greenwich Street. You walk with your brother to a small corner restaurant named Gregory's. It looks busy.

"Must be a good sign," Reid says. He nods to the crowd. "Empty restaurants are usually horrible."

You nod. Your mouth waters at the delicious smells wafting through the air. You're so hungry you can hardly stand it.

The two of you add your name to the waiting list. As you wait for a table, you hear something strange. It sounds like the roar of a jet plane flying low in the sky. A moment later there's a horrific noise. The whole world seems to shake.

To you it sounds like a crash, followed by an explosion. You and Reid look at each other.

"What was that?" Reid asks. He looks worried.

You step away from the building and look down Greenwich Street. In the distance, you see a huge plume of smoke rising from one of the towers of the World Trade Center.

To go see what's happening, turn to page 14.
To keep waiting for your table, turn to page 16.

Something is seriously wrong. You and Reid walk up the street and head further into the city. As you pass others, you see them looking up at the clouds of smoke.

"This isn't good," Reid says nervously. "Something big is happening."

Soon, the sound of sirens confirms it. There was an accident, but you're not sure what it is. Many people in their cars are looking to see what happened too.

Whatever happened was just a few blocks from you. The rest of the city seems just as curious, and maybe afraid, as you are.

Moments later you pass a woman walking in the opposite direction. Her hand covers her mouth. Streaks of tears trail down her face. Her head shakes as if she can't believe what she's seen.

"It was a plane," she tells a nearby woman. "But now it's gone. It's all gone!"

Did a plane just crash into one of the buildings? you wonder.

You tell yourself it must be an accident. Plane crashes happen. But how often do they hit buildings? Especially in the middle of a big city. It doesn't seem possible.

As you get closer to the scene, you hear more sirens. A New York City Fire Department ladder truck pushes through the crowded street. Taxis and cars move out of the way. You can see firefighters gearing up in the back of the truck. One of them steers the back end of the vehicle.

You and Reid turn left on Carlisle Street, then turn right on Washington. As you round the corner, you can't believe what you see.

Turn to page 19.

You realize there's nothing you can do. You're a tourist here and you'd only get in the way. If people are hurt, the emergency responders will take care of it.

You and Reid step off the curb and stand in the crowd with the others. People around you are talking. A middle-aged man in a black business suit rushes into the crowd. He seems frantic. Sweat pours down his face.

"A passenger plane just hit the North Tower!" he shouts. He's struggling to catch his breath.

"At the World Trade Center?" the restaurant hostess asks.

The man nods. He closes his eyes. He winces as though he's seeing the crash again and again. People are shouting and asking questions. He looks overwhelmed. You're having a hard time even hearing what people are asking.

"A plane hit one of the Twin Towers?" Reid cries, looking at you. "Seriously?"

You know very little about New York City. But you know the World Trade Center's twin towers are the tallest buildings in the city. They were the tallest in the country before the Sears Tower was built in downtown Chicago.

"Are there any survivors?" a teenage boy asks. Almost as soon as he says it, he seems to know the answer.

"No . . . no," the man replies, shaking his head. His mouth clenches up as if he's going to cry. "No way. The whole plane just exploded into a ball of fire and smoke and . . ."

The man covers his face. It's hard to imagine seeing something like that.

The restaurant is in chaos with the news. Everyone wants to know what happened.

Turn the page.

You don't really care about eating anymore. Your appetite is long gone. The city has been shaken by a terrible tragedy.

You and Reid decide to see what's happened for yourself. Maybe there's something you can do to help. You move through the crowded sidewalks and take a side street. When you turn right onto Washington Street, you're stunned by what you see.

The North Tower of the World Trade Center burns after being struck by a passenger plane

The towers of the World Trade Center rise into the sky about three blocks away. The South Tower stands unharmed. But a little further back, the North Tower tells a different story. Smoke billows from a giant flaming hole in the upper floors.

"Oh, my God," you whisper, barely able to blink. "It must've been a huge plane."

Chunks of debris drop from the burning tower. Papers flitter to the ground from the blazing hole. It looks like oversized confetti. But there's no parade in the streets below. There are people everywhere looking up in shock and horror.

Fire trucks scream by as they head to the scene. They screech to a stop next to the burning tower. Firefighters jump from the trucks carrying large bundles of firehose over their shoulders.

Turn the page.

You try and imagine how something like this could have happened. You think about the people in the plane and inside the building. You look at where the plane struck. There are a number of floors above the impact site.

How will they escape? you wonder.

"We have to do something," you whisper out loud.

Reid hears you and nods slowly. His face looks shocked.

"I'm not sure what can we do though," he says. "Should we check out the tower or let the emergency crews handle it?"

To let the first responders do their jobs, go to page 21.
To get a closer look at the North Tower, turn to page 24.

"We should stay put," you decide. "We'd only get in everyone's way."

Neither you nor Reid are trained to do any sort of rescue work. You're just a couple of tourists. You decide to stay. You both watch in horror as rescuers rush toward the scene.

Debris continues to fall to the ground from the burning skyscraper. You notice damage to some of the nearby buildings. It's hard to grasp how many people were hurt or killed from the crash. You can't believe the courage of the firefighters and other responders as they rush into the burning tower.

Just then, someone in the crowd shrieks and points.

"OH! Oh, NO!" a woman gasps, pointing up. "They're jumping!"

Turn the page.

Very briefly, you see someone throw them self from the hole in the North Tower. You quickly look away. But you'll never forget the image. Someone chose to jump to their death rather than die in the fire. And they're not the only one.

Other people around you gasp and shout. Others weep openly. People are leaning into each other for strength and support. Total strangers are coming together in a tragic situation.

Before long, you suddenly hear the roar and scream of airplane engines. When you glance up, you see another plane flying low—too low. It flies straight into the South Tower!

The explosion is deafening. A ball of flame and smoke billow out from the impact. Glass and chunks of the plane and building rain down nearby.

Everyone around you is screaming in terror. A man shouts above the crowd.

A fireball explodes as a second plane hits the South Tower

"Oh my God! Both towers! This is no accident!" he insists. "This was done on purpose!"

You can't believe what you're seeing. Every part of you is shaking. But you find it impossible to look away.

"We should get away from here!" Reid insists.

To stay and keep watching, turn to page 26.
To run for cover, turn to page 27.

"We can't just stand around and do nothing," you tell Reid.

Your older brother agrees. Together, you move closer to the scene and ask a firefighter if there's anything you can do.

"Get water from that store," a FDNY commander says, pointing. "Our crews are going to be hot and miserable."

You and Reid duck into the small convenience store across the street. You explain what is needed and the store owner nods. He lets you take packs of water bottles out to the crews. There are fire trucks parked everywhere. You hand water bottles to the sweaty and exhausted firefighters coming out of the buildings.

As you go back for more water, an injured woman falls down in front of you. She's holding her shoulder, which is bleeding badly.

No one seems to have noticed her. She's groaning in pain. It looks like she might've been hit by glass falling from the building.

"She needs help!" Reid exclaims. "It doesn't look good."

You aren't a doctor. You aren't sure how to help her. The firefighters are counting on you to get more water. You look around and see an ambulance about a block away.

To tend to the injured woman yourself, turn to page 29.
To lead her to the ambulance, turn to page 31.

You're too stunned by the horrible sight to do anything. It feels like you're frozen in place. You're not alone. The people crowding the street near you are doing the same thing. No one can believe what's happening. One plane hitting a major building in New York is tragic. But planes hitting both towers of the World Trade Center? That's no coincidence.

The United States is under attack before your eyes. The thought of two planes full of people crashing to their deaths is more than you can stomach.

As you watch the chaos unfold before you, pieces of metal and glass continue to rain down. Suddenly, a giant chunk of the destroyed plane whistles down toward you. You have no time to react before it strikes you.

THE END

To follow another path, turn to page 9.
To learn more about the events of September 11, 2001, turn to page 103.

"Come on! We have to get out of here!" Reid shouts.

He's pulling at your arm. You feel numb with fear and shock but manage to look your brother in the eye. Tears are streaming down his face. You realize you're crying too.

"This isn't over yet," Reid cries. "If this is the work of terrorists, they might just be getting started."

You nod, slowly pulling yourself back to reality. The city is under attack, and you're stuck in the middle of it. Who knows what might happen next? You're unsure where to go. You're in Manhattan, an island within New York City. Getting off the island might be difficult.

Reid pulls you away and you follow. Glass and chunks of metal are falling from the sky. A piece of paper blows up against your leg.

Turn the page.

The paper looks like a printout of numbers and data. It's probably paperwork from the offices in the South Tower. It shouldn't be out here in the street.

You leave the destruction of the World Trade Center behind you. Emergency vehicles and first responders rush in the opposite direction.

You walk for almost an hour before hearing a low rumble. When you look back, you see that one of the towers is no longer standing. The South Tower has collapsed. All you see in the distance is smoke and a growing dust cloud. You're still in the city, but you've escaped.

You're grateful to be alive. But you'll never forget what you've seen.

THE END

To follow another path, turn to page 9.
To learn more about the events of September 11, 2001, turn to page 103.

The woman is bleeding heavily. You don't know if you'll be able to get her help in time.

"Here," you tell the woman. "Let us help you."

You pull off your sweatshirt and rip off one of the sleeves. You press the material into her wound. She winces, but you're able to stop the blood flow. Using another piece of fabric, you tie it tight to hold it there. Reid goes and finds a paramedic.

As he does, there's a screech in the sky. You look up in time to see another plane flying low overhead. People scream as it crashes into the South Tower. It disintegrates into a ball of fire and smoke. Both towers have been hit within a half hour of each other!

Reid rushes back with two paramedics and a stretcher. The woman thanks you as they carry her away.

Turn the page.

People around you are shouting that the plane crashes are no accident. Many believe it is the work of terrorists. You think they might be right.

You continue to help the firefighters by guiding people to the ambulance. Almost an hour passes when something even more unthinkable happens.

You hear a loud rumbling sound from above, followed by the screams of people around you. You look up to see that the South Tower is beginning to collapse. A cloud of dust surrounds the skyscraper as it collapses, one floor at a time.

"We have to run!" Reid shouts. "We're too close!"

But they still need our help, you think.

To stay and keep helping the first responders, turn to page 33.

To run and hide from the falling debris, turn to page 34.

You're not a medical professional. You don't know how to stop the woman's bleeding. Thankfully, the paramedics at the ambulance should.

"Let us help you," you tell the woman.

She grimaces in pain as you and Reid help her up. Together, you carry her to the ambulance. Her shoulder is bleeding badly. You hope you're not too late.

The paramedics are overwhelmed at the ambulance. There are a lot of injured people. But there's nothing more you can do. You leave the woman near the ambulance and hope they can help her.

As you wonder if you could've done more to help, you hear a loud screech above you. You look up and see another plane flying low.

Turn the page.

Before you can react, you see it smash into the middle part of the South Tower. Like the first plane, it explodes in a flash of fire and smoke.

Large chunks of the building smash down on the streets around you. One of them crushes the ambulance and the people inside. Paramedics scramble way, pulling patients with them.

You run away, then realize Reid isn't with you. When you turn, you can see he's face down on the ground near a big chunk of the wrecked plane. Your brother isn't moving. He's become another victim of the 9/11 attacks.

THE END

To follow another path, turn to page 9.
To learn more about the events of September 11, 2001, turn to page 103.

You want to stay with the first responders. But they start to run from the collapsing building. A wave of dust and debris heads your way. You have no choice but to run too.

Soon the dust surrounds you. It's so thick that it's impossible to breathe. You're coughing hard. The dust irritates your eyes. It hurts to open them.

You've become another patient. Eventually, you and your brother find help. As the paramedics wash out your eyes, you wonder how much damage the dust has done to your lungs.

Years later, you find out. Both you and Reid have lung cancer. You learn that nearly 10,000 first responders were diagnosed with cancer as well. Although you survived the attacks on 9/11, you're slowly dying from being so close to it.

THE END

To follow another path, turn to page 9.
To learn more about the events of September 11, 2001, turn to page 103.

Reid is right. Staying here is a terrible idea. You both run as fast as possible from the rapidly approaching cloud of dust and debris. Reid covers his mouth and is squinting. You use the remains of your sweatshirt to cover your own mouth. You see others fleeing and shouting in terror. As you approach a pizza joint, you have an idea.

A cloud of choking dust rolls into the city streets after a tower collapses

"Reid!" you shout. "Over there!"

You both dash into the small restaurant. It's crowded with others who had the same idea. You close the door behind you, hearing the bells on the door jingle. A moment later, the front window turns completely dark with dust and dirt. You can hear debris tinkling against the shop's window.

The people inside the pizzeria are moaning and weeping. It's hard to believe an entire skyscraper came down so close to you. You think of all the people trapped in the upper floors. There's little hope that any of them survived.

Although you found cover, you're completely caked in dust. Tears cut clean lines down people's dirty faces. The horrific events have taken a toll on everyone. In time, the dust settles and you can see outside again. But you're almost afraid to leave.

To keep helping people outside, turn to page 36.
To get as far from the disaster as possible, turn to page 38.

If there are any first responders still around, they're going to need help. You take a deep breath and go out to do whatever you can. It isn't easy. Many people are injured. The firefighters are exhausted and thirsty. You and Reid check other stores for water. Some of the owners offer food to bring to the exhausted workers.

About a half hour after the South Tower falls, another tragedy happens. You watch in horror as the North Tower begins to collapse. You watch as giant chunks of the building fall and smash fire trucks. People are running for their lives—including you and Reid.

Like last time, you duck into a store to wait out the cloud of dust and debris. You feel like you're living in a nightmare. Two planes have crashed into two of the world's most iconic buildings. And now, they're both just—gone. There's nothing left but huge piles of twisted metal and rubble.

Firefighters search for survivors in the destruction of the World Trade Center

Broken, bruised, and exhausted, you and Reid continue to assist the first responders. It's tough work, but you feel a little better knowing you're doing something to help.

THE END

To follow another path, turn to page 9.
To learn more about the events of September 11, 2001, turn to page 103.

You're not sure you can take much more tragedy. You and Reid feel like you've done enough. You both decide to head away from the World Trade Center. Unfortunately, New York's worst day isn't quite over.

As you walk through the debris-covered streets, you hear a familiar rumbling noise. You're almost afraid to look, but you do. The North Tower of the World Trade Center is collapsing! Like its twin, the tower comes down in a matter of seconds. And just like before, there's a huge wave of dust coming toward you.

You and Reid run and look for another place to hide. But the blinding cloud of dust is too quick this time. As you cross the street to duck into a T-shirt shop, the last thing you hear is the rumbling sound of an engine.

A large truck, hoping to get clear of the destruction, has rammed into you. You're thrown dozens of feet through the air and land hard on the street. The last thing you see is your brother's horrified, dust-covered face as your world goes black.

THE END

To follow another path, turn to page 9.
To learn more about the events of September 11, 2001, turn to page 103.

Huge piles of rubble smoldered for many days after the attacks on the World Trade Center.

CHAPTER 3

NORTH TOWER OF TERROR

When you get to work on Tuesday, September 11, you're just happy it's not Monday. As you greet your office coworkers, your friend Amy points at your head.

"Tell me you didn't pay for that haircut," Amy says.

You instinctively put your hand to your hair. As you do, a smile spreads across her face. She shakes her head and laughs.

Turn the page.

"I'm kidding," she says. "But your reaction is priceless."

You and Amy head to your desks after she grabs some coffee. You're both in a little earlier than usual. There's a meeting at 9:00 a.m. and you have numbers to review first. Your boss, Dale, has an incredible way of catching errors, no matter how small.

You've been working in the North Tower of the World Trade Center for almost seven years. After all this time, you still haven't gotten used to the view from the 80th floor. It's still breathtaking to see the city spread out below you. With the sun shining and few clouds in the sky—it's almost magical.

"You paying attention?" Amy asks. She's pointing at her computer monitor where the year-to-date numbers are highlighted.

As you turn from the window to answer her, you hear a loud screeching sound. You look up to see what looks like the shadow of a giant bird outside. An instant later, there's a giant explosion! It blows you and Amy out of your chairs. Glass and smoke are everywhere. You can hear people shouting and screaming.

Amy looks dazed, lying on her side. Everything around you turns chaotic. Fire is burning in places on the ceiling.

Your first instinct is to escape and get out. Is it safe to leave? You look around. You see several coworkers who need help. Maybe it's best to wait for rescue workers to arrive. They'll be able to help the injured and get you to safety.

To wait for help from rescuers, turn to page 44.
To escape immediately, turn to page 45.

When you sit up, you quickly glance outside. Chunks of the building fall past the windows. It's like a bomb exploded a few floors above you.

"Amy!" you call out and crawl over to your friend.

"What happened?" Amy murmurs. She's a little out of it.

"Not sure," you say. "But there's a fire and we're going to wait for help."

"Fire, fire!" a woman shouts. You glance over and see the main doors to the elevator lobby are open. Flames are blazing there, melting the carpet and peeling the wallpaper.

Over near the south meeting room, Dale and some visitors are bleeding too.

To help Dale and the others, turn to page 47.

To try and put the fire out before it spreads, turn to page 49.

Everything in your mind is screaming: ESCAPE! You crawl over to Amy. She's dazed from the blast.

"Hey," you tell Amy. "We have to get you up. We're getting out of here!"

"What happened?" Amy asks.

"It was a plane! A passenger plane," Sheeda, one of the accountants, shouts. "I saw it coming in low and it . . . it just . . ."

You can't wrap your head around that. *Did a plane full of people fly into our building?* All of those people on board—dead in an instant. It's too horrible to even think about.

You stand up on wobbly legs. Fires burn above you. The ceiling tiles are melting away rapidly as the flames spread. When you get your balance, you help Amy to her feet.

Turn the page.

Black smoke pours from the burning top floors of the North Tower

"We need to find a way out of here," you whisper to Amy. "And fast."

You and Amy try several stairwells and finally find one that seems safe. Nine flights down, you see a man sitting on a landing. He's a larger man who's out of breath. Amy urges you to hurry.

To help the man to safety, turn to page 51.
To leave the man and escape, turn to page 53.

There's no way you can leave the others behind. You and Amy work to help them. You see that the fire is spreading, so you move to another part of the office. You wonder if firefighters will arrive in time to help everyone out.

People are talking about what happened. An accountant named Sheeda speaks up.

"I saw the plane," she says. Her eyes are wild with fear. "It crashed into the building!"

"So, it was an accident?" Dale asks. "Something must've happened to the pilot."

Not everyone is so sure. A few even think it was done on purpose.

People try to call their loved ones. You want to call your sister, but the phone lines are down. Even those with cell phones are having trouble. Dale closes his flip phone in frustration. He can't get a signal.

Turn the page.

The heat from the fire feels closer. The flames are spreading. Just as you're about to suggest everyone try the stairs, you see something unbelievable.

Through the window, you see another plane flying low. Before you can shout in terror, the plane steers into the South Tower. It explodes into a ball of flame. You feel the building shake from the explosion. The windows rattle and a few of them crack. Chunks of building and debris rain down from floors higher up.

These crashes are no accident! You want to escape—now! Dale seems to think the group should wait for help.

To leave Dale and make your escape, turn to page 55.

To convince Dale and the others to come with you, turn to page 56.

You hope to stop the fire before it spreads. You tell Amy you'll be right back. People are shouting and screaming. No one knows when the fire department will arrive.

You pass a metal box in the hallway. Quickly, you pull out the fire extinguisher. You've never used one before, but it seems pretty simple—just pull the pin and squeeze the handle.

Turn the page.

Fire extinguisher

You dash to the elevator lobby. Searing flames are everywhere. You squeeze the handle and aim for the base of the fire. You manage to knock down some of the flames, but the fire quickly flares up again. It's everywhere and spreading quickly.

The air is thick with smoke. Trying to battle the blaze is impossible. You cough and your eyes burn from the heat. Your skin feels ready to blister as the temperature rises by the second.

As your extinguisher runs out of juice, a strange scent hits your nose. It almost smells like fuel.

Is that from the plane? you wonder.

In the next moment there's an explosion. You see a momentary flash. And then—nothing but darkness.

THE END

To follow another path, turn to page 9.
To learn more about the events of September 11, 2001, turn to page 103.

"Hey buddy," you say to the man. He's got his head in his hands and he's sweating a lot. "You need some help?"

The man looks up. "Just leave me," the man says. "I . . . I can't make it."

Amy hits you on the shoulder. She's pointing up the stairwell. There's fire spreading down the stairwell rapidly. Then you smell fumes. You're not sure where it's coming from, but it's making you worry. It could be fuel from the plane.

"We don't have much time," Amy warns. "We need to move."

"You go on ahead," you say to Amy. "I'm going to help . . . what's your name, pal?"

"Albert," the man says. "I'm Albert."

Amy looks like she doesn't want to leave you, but she does. In moments she's disappeared down the stairs.

Turn the page.

You work to get Albert on his feet. He's a big guy, but after a few tries, he's standing up.

"Where are the firefighters?" Albert asks.

"I'm sure they're on their way," you say, feeling heat from the approaching fire. "I don't think the elevators are working."

"They're not," Albert says. "They're all out."

As you struggle to help Albert down the stairs, he mumbles something else.

"This was no accident," Albert says. "This had to be an act of terrorism."

Before you can ask him how he knows, the fire has caught up to you. There was no way to outrun it. Although your actions were heroic, you and Albert meet a fiery end.

THE END

To follow another path, turn to page 9.
To learn more about the events of September 11, 2001, turn to page 103.

You feel bad leaving the man behind, but the fire is coming fast. You and Amy are running for your lives. A pair of firefighters are running up the stairs. They look exhausted.

The fire is soon at your backs. You try a door on the 45th floor. Thankfully, it opens. Maybe escaping onto another floor will keep you safe.

"We have to find another stairwell," you tell Amy. "One that isn't on fire."

You both run into an unfamiliar office space. There are people gathered around, trying to determine what to do.

"You all need to get out, now!" you shout. "The fire is spreading!"

They ask questions, but you don't wait to answer them. You're already running toward another stairwell. As you pull open another door, you hear a gigantic boom somewhere nearby.

Turn the page.

"What was that?" Amy asks. It sounded like another bomb hit.

The two of you run down the stairwell, jumping down three steps at a time. You weave between people who are moving too slowly. After what seems like forever, you exit the North Tower's lobby onto the street.

You see rubble and debris everywhere. Flames and smoke are streaming from a gaping wound in the side of the tower.

"It's coming down!" someone shouts.

You look up to see the top of the tower beginning to crumble. You've managed to escape the North Tower. But the nightmare of this day has only just begun.

THE END

To follow another path, turn to page 9.
To learn more about the events of September 11, 2001, turn to page 103.

"I don't think the fire department is going to get here in time," you tell Amy and the others. "I'm leaving!"

"You don't know what's out there!" Dale shouts.

"We'll die if we stay here!" you shout back.

Before anyone can stop you, you and Amy run away from the group. You try the stairs to see if any of them are safe. People are streaming down, desperate to escape. The stairwells are packed.

The toxic smoke is quickly filling the area. The fire is spreading fast. You and Amy wedge your way into the stairwell. The movement is slow going. It's taking way too long to get anywhere.

At the 64th floor, Amy pulls you aside. "The fire is way above us," Amy says. "We should be safe until help comes."

To wait for rescue here, turn to page 58.
To keep going down the stairs, turn to page 60.

"The fire is spreading fast!" you shout. "We need to get out of here or we'll all burn to death!"

Your words put fear into your coworkers. Even Dale seems ready to listen. Miguel, an account executive, nods.

"It's true," he says. "The fire department might not get to us in time. They've never fought a fire like this before."

Everyone agrees to leave. You and Amy lead the group across the floor. You try some of the stairwell doors. Many of them are jammed shut. One is blocked with a huge chunk of concrete.

At long last, you find an unlocked stairwell door. When you open it, you find it's packed with people.

One by one, your group merges in with the other North Tower employees. It's slow moving, but you make your way down floor after floor.

Dark, narrow stairs made escaping the burning towers difficult.

Eventually, somewhere around the 48th level, firefighters pass by you. You're amazed. They're going up while everyone else is going down.

Sometime later, you hear a loud rumble and feel the building quiver.

"That's not good," Amy gasps. Everyone instinctively looks up. You can't see any fire.

At the next landing, you find Miguel off to the side. He's clutching his ankle and wincing in pain.

To help Miguel down the stairs, turn to page 62.
To keep going, turn to page 65.

"We're far enough away," you say, agreeing with Amy. "It'll take a long time before it reaches us."

Amy nods. "Hopefully the firefighters can knock it down soon."

You open the door to another floor of office space. Other than scattered papers and tipped-over chairs, it's empty. It looks like the workers here made a frantic escape.

You both walk to the window to see what's happening outside. You get a good view of the South Tower. It's burning, and papers are fluttering down like confetti.

"I can't believe this is happening," Amy whispers. She presses her hands against the window.

The two of you wait and watch, hopeful for rescue. But soon, something happens that takes your breath away.

The South Tower begins to collapse, straight down like an accordion. Floor after floor gives way beneath the weight. A ring of dust and smoke chases the wreckage down to the city streets.

"NO!" you shout. You can't believe what you've just seen.

"Wait. If the South Tower collapsed, that means . . ." Amy begins.

"Ours might be next," you whisper, finishing her thought.

The two of you run to the stairwell, but it's too late. The stairs are packed. At floor 64, you're still high up. You'll never make it down in time. Half an hour later, the North Tower collapses, burying you and everyone else inside in seconds.

THE END

To follow another path, turn to page 9.
To learn more about the events of September 11, 2001, turn to page 103.

"Maybe you're right," you say. "But I don't want to take the risk. We should keep going."

Amy shakes her head. She's worn out and exhausted. She tells you there's no way she can keep going. You offer to carry her down, but she smiles and refuses.

"There's no way you'd be able to do that," she says. "If anything, I could carry you, if I wasn't so tired."

You hate to leave her behind, but she's stubborn.

"I'll see you when this is over," she says, and disappears through the door to the 64th floor.

You continue down the stairs. At some point, you see firefighters struggling to make their way up. You can't help but marvel at their bravery.

We're running out of a burning building, you think. *And they're running IN!*

The progress on the stairs is slow, and it's making you nervous. At some point, there's a large rumble, and the building seems to shake. You're not sure what it is. It makes the stream of people in the staircase move faster.

Eventually you emerge outside. Through clouds of thick dust, you're shocked to see the South Tower is completely gone. You think things can't possibly get worse. But then they do.

The ground rumbles. You look up to see the North Tower is beginning to collapse too. You think about Amy and the others still trapped inside. But all you can do is run for your life.

THE END

To follow another path, turn to page 9.
To learn more about the events of September 11, 2001, turn to page 103.

"C'mon Miguel," you say, extending your hand. "Let me help you."

Miguel refuses a few times, but you insist. You're not taking no for an answer. Amy keeps going, along with your other coworkers. Amy and the others wish you luck. They look at you like they may never see you again.

You wrap your arm around Miguel's back and throw his arm around your shoulder. You wedge your way into the flow of people descending the stairs. It's slow going. You're upsetting the people behind you.

Just ignore them, you think. *We all just want to get out of this alive.*

Miguel winces every few steps. There was no way he would've made it down on his own. You just know that as long as you can stay ahead of the fire, you should be okay.

Then you hear some startling news from someone passing by.

"The South Tower completely collapsed!" a man with a goatee says to a woman.

That must have been the big rumble we heard, you think.

You look at Miguel and his face says it all. He also heard what the man said.

"It doesn't mean our tower will fall," you say to him. "But we have to keep moving, just in case."

It seems to take forever, but you finally reach the bottom floor. But before you can reach for the stairwell door, you hear an enormous rumble all around you. People in the stairwell are screaming as the entire North Tower collapses.

When you open your eyes, you're not sure how much time has passed. You just know you're alive.

Turn the page.

You and Miguel ducked under the stairway just as the walls collapsed around you. Thankfully, the stairwell formed a pocket to protect you. A short time later, you hear voices.

"We've got two survivors!" a rescue worker shouts. "Easy now, we've got you."

You're broken and bruised, but you're going to live.

And thanks to you, so will Miguel.

THE END

To follow another path, turn to page 9.
To learn more about the events of September 11, 2001, turn to page 103.

It feels awful to leave Miguel behind, but you don't have a choice. He'll only slow you down . . . and everyone behind you.

"The firefighters will be here soon," you tell Miguel, putting a comforting hand on his shoulder. You're not sure if they'll get to him, but you hope they will.

Miguel nods and waves you off. "Go on," he says. "When it's my time, it's my time."

His words send shivers down your spine. You keep moving down the stairs but feel awful.

After about 20 minutes, you've reached the bottom. Everyone from your office is outside and heading away from the building.

You're all shocked to see that the South Tower is gone. It's as if it was stomped into a massive pile of rubble.

Turn the page.

The South Tower collapsed 56 minutes after being struck by the plane.

Is the North Tower next? you wonder. Then you tell yourself, *No, it should be fine. After all, this tower was hit first and it's still standing.*

You've done what you could to get your friends and coworkers out. But could you do more?

To leave the North Tower behind, go to page 67.

To help the first responders near the entrance, turn to page 68.

You managed to escape the North Tower. You don't want to push your luck. So, you decide the best thing to do is to keep moving.

You look around. Many people are covered in thick dust. Multiple fire trucks and ambulances have been crushed by falling debris. No one knew any of this was coming. No one ever thought the South Tower would collapse.

As you make your way down the street, the unthinkable happens again. You feel a deep rumbling beneath your feet. You look up in horror to see the North Tower beginning to collapse. A ring of smoke and dust circles the skyscraper. It's coming down, just like its twin.

You don't have time to think. All you can do is run.

THE END

To follow another path, turn to page 9.
To learn more about the events of September 11, 2001, turn to page 103.

You can't just hang around here while others are helping the injured. Despite Amy's protests, you run back toward the North Tower. You ask the paramedics if there's anything you can do.

One of them has you hold a bag of saline solution as they insert a needle in a patient's arm. Another asks you to hold gauze against the victim's wounds.

Those who can walk move toward a nearby ambulance. Soon you're tasked with pushing a stretcher carrying a man with severe burns. As you navigate the cluttered sidewalks, you feel a deep, terrible rumble. You look up to see that the North Tower is collapsing!

A brown ring of dust and smoke rapidly falls toward you, crumbling each floor as it goes. You take off running, pushing the stretcher ahead of you to try to get the burned man to safety.

Rubble and thick clouds of dust fill the streets of New York after the towers collapse

But the building's collapse is too quick. You and the burn victim are crushed beneath the weight of the tower's ruins. You did what you could, but fate had other plans for you.

THE END

To follow another path, turn to page 9.
To learn more about the events of September 11, 2001, turn to page 103.

CHAPTER 4

RESCUE: IMPOSSIBLE

Today started out like any other. You're at the fire station with the rest of your crew. You trash talk each other, do equipment checks, and keep busy until the next call comes in.

The sun is shining. It's a beautiful day in New York City. You're sitting on the back bumper of the Number 4 ladder truck, talking with your partner, Kurt Holmgren.

"I'm telling you, Wiley snores like a hibernating bear," Kurt says. He's rubbing his tired eyes.

Turn the page.

"That's wild," you say, tapping the clipboard against your leg. "I didn't hear a thing."

Kurt shakes his head. "You'd sleep through a hurricane, pal," he says. "I envy you."

You and the crew are due to perform hose testing today. "We'd better get started," you say. "Or we'll hear about it from the chief."

As you look at the clipboard to see which truck is first, a call comes in.

"Yes!" Kurt says. "Sounds like our lucky day."

You laugh. "We're just putting off the pain," you reply. "This will be waiting for us when we get back."

The call is for a smell of gas at a pizza shop on Fulton Street. Chief Baldwin, Kurt, Tony Wiley, and you hop on a truck and drive to the scene. The call ends up like another you went to this morning—no one finds anything.

But as you're standing there, you hear a screech of engines in the sky. You look up to see a commercial airplane fly into the North Tower of the World Trade Center. The plane explodes instantly, creating a ball of flame on the skyscraper's upper levels. Debris falls to the ground as fire roars in the gaping hole.

Your crew members are shouting and are as shocked as you are. Everyone immediately runs to the truck and climbs aboard. The World Trade Center is only blocks away, but it seems like the longest drive ever. You've never faced anything like this. The chief is assigning what you'll do on the scene.

To work with the engineer and get hose lines set up, turn to page 74.

To get geared up to enter the North Tower, turn to page 76.

The chief makes a call to get every firehouse in the area to respond. But your small crew will get things started since you're already so close.

"I need someone to work with Wiley to get some water on the tower," the chief says.

You volunteer. Wiley will run the pump while you get the hose lines going. You connect the hose to the building's fire department connection. That will provide water to the sprinkler systems inside the North Tower.

Firefighters work to put out a fire at the World Trade Center

You hope it works. But you have no idea if the sprinklers are still working or not.

Soon, crews from other stations start to arrive. The area below the North Tower is filled with fire trucks and firefighters carrying their gear. Many carry tools such as pike poles or bundles of firehose. Others carry Halligans. These heavy tools can pry open doors and pull down flaming ceilings.

"The elevators are out," you hear one man say. "We're in for a long climb."

People are emerging from the building. Some are injured and are bleeding. They look confused about where to go. Debris is still falling from the tower. You know these people need help. But the fire needs to be controlled too.

To help people who are leaving the building, turn to page 78.

To get water on the building to control the fire, turn to page 80.

You slip your arms into the shoulder straps of your air tank, or SCBA. It's on a rack in the back of your seat. You pull the cord to release it and then tighten the straps. Within a few minutes, you're ready to go inside the building.

Wiley pulls the pumper truck up near the closest hydrant and you jump off.

You and Kurt help Wiley get water to the truck and connect to the fire department connection at the base of the building. You wonder if the sprinkler system is even working at all.

Once water is flowing, Kurt opens a side panel on the truck, and the two of you pull out some gear. You grab a heavy Halligan tool, used for prying open doors, and a bundle of hose. Kurt grabs an axe and another bundle of hose.

"Word is the elevators are out," the chief says. "You two ready to get your steps in?"

You and Kurt nod.

You're used to the weight on your back and shoulders. But you don't know how you'll feel after climbing up so many levels of stairs. It's hard to tell what floor was hit. It looks like it's somewhere above the 80th level.

"You two are my eyes and ears until the others get here," Chief Baldwin says. "Radio back and let us know how things are looking."

You and Kurt nod and run toward the entrance. There are already people coming out. Some of them look banged up. You prepare yourself for a long climb.

"We should check the elevators," Kurt says. "If one's still working, we can get up there quicker."

He has a point. But the stairs would be safer.

To head to the nearest stairwell, turn to page 82.
To check the elevators, turn to page 84.

Someone is going to get hit with falling debris, you think, watching the confusion in their faces.

"Everyone!" you shout. "I need you to clear out of here. Move away from the tower!"

The people are looking up, confused. You realize that some of them have no idea what happened. They're pointing up at the smoke and the fire high up on the North Tower.

You lead the survivors away from the building toward ambulances parked a block away. A chunk of metal and concrete slams down on the pavement near where they were just standing. It startles everyone, and they move away quickly.

You look back toward the building's entrance. The officers from the different fire houses are setting up their command center in the lobby. They're dispatching firefighters to the different stairwells and trying to come up with a plan.

Falling rubble was dangerous and deadly for people on the street.

After leading the victims to the ambulances, you head back to the burning tower. But on the way, you're struck by another huge chunk of falling debris. Your helmet and gear aren't enough to save you. You're a hero for helping get others to safety. But you've become a casualty in the process.

THE END

To follow another path, turn to page 9.
To learn more about the events of September 11, 2001, turn to page 103.

As a firefighter, you know you're not supposed to leave your post. Although this is unlike any fire scene you've ever been on, you need to stay focused. Firefighters who do their own thing sometimes end up getting themselves or others hurt or killed.

You work with guys from another station to spray water and foam up as high as you can. It's doing nothing for the fires high up in the tower, but hopefully the foam will keep it from spreading.

You next help Wiley set up a relay line to another pumper. When you're about to make the connection, you hear a familiar screech of jet engines overhead. Then, although you can't see it, you hear another deafening explosion.

"Another plane!" a voice crackles through your radio. "South Tower, South Tower!"

The people gathered on the street scream and shout. Some are pointing to the sky.

Huge flames erupt after the second plane hits the South Tower

One plane hitting a skyscraper could be a terrible accident. But two planes within a half hour of each other? There's more going on here than just freak accidents.

You look up to see chunks of debris from the South Tower raining down.

Our trucks are going to get destroyed, you think. *If that happens, we're in trouble.*

To move a truck out of harm's way, turn to page 86.
To continue working where you are, turn to page 88.

"I don't like it," you say.

You have a bad feeling about the elevators. There's a reason Chief Baldwin said they were out.

"All right," Kurt says. "Let's get to climbing."

The two of you find a staircase that seems stable. You begin the long climb, moving as quickly as you can with all of your gear. It's like carrying half of a person with you. You've trained for this, so it's not impossible. But you wonder how you'll feel at floor 30, 40, or even 50.

You're passing people as they head down the stairs. They look confused and scared. You're not sure how far down they've come.

There's a lot of chatter on the radios. You hear command trying to coordinate rescue and fire suppression efforts. Somewhere around the 32nd floor, the stairwell rumbles. Both you and Kurt stop at the next landing.

"What was that?" Kurt shouts. He's trying to peer up the stairwell to see if there's something wrong.

You listen in on the radio and can't believe what you're hearing.

"Another plane!" you gasp. "It hit the South Tower."

"You've got to be kidding me," Kurt says. "How? What is going on?"

You're beginning to think none of this is an accident. The odds are impossible.

You suddenly see a woman with severe burns coming down the stairs. She doesn't look good and falls down. Some of the other North Tower workers help her up.

To help the burned woman, turn to page 90.

To have the others help her and keep climbing, turn to page 92.

You're not sure it's safe, but you decide to try the elevators anyway. You and Kurt run to the elevator banks. Amazingly, one of them is working.

"Jackpot," Kurt says. "We'll take this up and save ourselves a ton of time."

You stand there for a moment, waiting for the elevator to arrive. When it does, you nod. If you can avoid climbing up all those stairs, you'll have the strength and energy to do some good.

You join Kurt on the elevator. He presses the button for 75. The doors close and you feel the car begin to rise. As it does, you pull out your facemask. You remove your helmet and pull the fireproof hood over your head. You don't know what to expect when the elevator door opens.

But then the elevator stops around the 60th floor, and the door stays closed.

"Oh boy, this isn't good," Kurt says. He pushes several buttons, but they're all dark. A moment later, the light inside the elevator car flickers off. You both turn on the flashlights hanging from the front of your turnout jackets.

"I'll pry the door," you say. You wedge the end of your Halligan between the closed inner doors. They open easily. You do the same for the outer doors. As soon as you do, you smell fumes—jet fuel!

A moment later, fire races down the elevator shaft in an explosion. The elevator car and cable are destroyed, sending you and Kurt crashing down to your doom.

THE END

To follow another path, turn to page 9.
To learn more about the events of September 11, 2001, turn to page 103.

I need to get these trucks moved, you think.

You abandon your post and run to Pumper #7. Wiley is at the pump panel wearing hearing protectors. He's keeping his eye on the pressure levels to make sure the hose lines have enough pressure to keep water and foam moving.

"Wiley!" you shout. "We need to move the truck. Chunks of the buildings are crashing down all around us!"

The engineer pulls his ear protection aside.

"Can't do it," Wiley says. "I'd have to take it out of pump gear and disconnect and—"

But Wiley doesn't finish what's he's saying. A large chunk of steel crashes down on Pumper #7. It nearly crushes the back half of the truck. Supply hoses snap from their connection, sending water everywhere. Flying debris hits you and Wiley, knocking you off of your feet.

A fire truck that was crushed by falling rubble from the towers

You fall to the pavement. At least your helmet protected your head. But you feel like the rest of your body has been crushed. Wiley is lying face down in a growing puddle of water. He's not moving, and you can't move either.

More debris falls around you. The last thing you feel is a pair of strong hands tugging you away. You close your eyes to the chaos, and sadly, never open them again.

THE END

To follow another path, turn to page 9.
To learn more about the events of September 11, 2001, turn to page 103.

There's nothing you can do about the trucks. Besides, there's a whole network of hoses connecting them to the building. There isn't time to disconnect it all to move anything. You remind yourself that "freelancing" on the job is another word for trouble. And there's enough trouble all around you as it is.

You watch as people continue streaming out of the North Tower. You also see the command group divide themselves up to tackle the South Tower crash. Everyone is spread thin. You think about Kurt and wonder where he ended up.

Did he get to the fire? Is there even any chance it can be put out?

Just then, a mass of steel and concrete falls from the South Tower nearby. It crushes the back end of an ambulance. You look away, unsure if there was a patient or anyone else in the back. If there was, you doubt they survived.

You keep working at pumping water and foam as you hear a sickening rumble. You look up to see a new horror. The South Tower is collapsing! A ring of toxic dust, smoke, and debris is cascading toward the ground. Everyone runs, including you and your crew.

As the wreckage of the skyscraper rains down, you're struck and knocked unconscious. You wake up in a hospital later that day. You did the best you could. You don't feel like it was enough. But for now, all you can do is heal.

THE END

To follow another path, turn to page 9.
To learn more about the events of September 11, 2001, turn to page 103.

You can't imagine letting the injured woman go by without helping her.

"I'm going to call it in," you tell Kurt.

You call in to command and let them know you've found an injured woman. You request someone meet her halfway down the stairwell.

"Negative, Team 1," the commander responds. "EMS is spread thin down here."

"Copy that," you say. You want to throw your radio against the wall in frustration. You want to help people but aren't able to.

"What's the plan?" Kurt asks.

"You keep going," you tell Kurt. "I'll help her."

Kurt's face says he doesn't like that plan. You're not supposed to split up with your partner when in a fire. You're supposed to stick together so you both leave the scene alive.

But this is different, you tell yourself. *We've never had a fire like this.*

You lift the woman up and she screams from her injuries. You carry her down with you, leaving Kurt behind. When you finally reach the ground, you hand her off to some paramedics.

A short time later, you watch in horror as the South Tower collapses. The command staff calls a Mayday for anyone in the North Tower. You're not sure Kurt will get out in time. Thirty minutes later, the North Tower collapses too. You never see your friend and partner again.

THE END

To follow another path, turn to page 9.
To learn more about the events of September 11, 2001, turn to page 103.

You stop a middle-aged guy coming down the stairs.

"Hey there," you say. "I need you to help this injured woman get downstairs."

The man looks scared to death, but he nods. He puts her arm around his shoulder and helps her down the stairs. You and Kurt continue moving up the stairs.

"Bless you brave men," an older woman says as you pass by. "We're going down to escape the fire. But you're heading up to face it."

You nod and think about what that means. You're willing to risk your life to help as many people as you can. But you don't feel like a hero. It's just part of the job.

The people coming downstairs are looking worse and worse. They're bleeding, burned, and in shock. You're almost afraid to see what's up there.

As you continue climbing, you feel the stairs rumble beneath your boots. The people coming down the stairs hold onto the railings. Some of them are screaming. A crackling voice over the radio raises goosebumps on your sweaty skin.

"South Tower is down!" someone shouts.

All you can think is, *What do they mean South Tower is down? Did it collapse? That's impossible!*

A second later a loud tone sounds through the radio. It's the sound no firefighter ever wants to hear.

"They're calling a Mayday!" you shout to Kurt. "South Tower came down. This one might be next!"

A Mayday means you need to get out—NOW! You feel frozen with panic.

To keep climbing to help more people, turn to page 94.

To head down the stairs as fast as possible, turn to page 96.

There are too many people still coming down the stairs. You feel like turning around is wrong. People still need help.

"We have to get out of here," Kurt says. "Let's drop our gear and bolt. We can't help anyone if we're dead."

Kurt has a point. But you can't do it. There might be someone up higher who still needs help. If you get to them, maybe you can help them down the stairs. If you can save even one more life, you'll be able to look at yourself in the mirror tomorrow.

"I'm going up," you tell Kurt. "This building was hit first and is still standing. I don't think it's going down."

You're not sure you believe it yourself, but you have to. Kurt nods. He knows the best chance of surviving is by sticking together.

Firefighters search for survivors in the wreckage of the fallen towers

You continue to climb, getting close to the fire. But a short time later you hear a thunderous rumbling from above. You stop and put your head down as the North Tower collapses around you and Kurt. Neither of you are heard from again.

THE END

To follow another path, turn to page 9.
To learn more about the events of September 11, 2001, turn to page 103.

"We need to go," you tell Kurt. "Now!"

You and Kurt join the thinning numbers of people evacuating the building. You both dump the bundles of firehose you've been carrying. That helps you move faster.

Step after step feels like seconds ticking by on a time bomb. You don't know if the North Tower will fall like its twin did. You just know you can't take that chance. You can't help but think of the people you were heading upstairs to rescue.

How many people are still up there? you wonder. *Did they even have a chance?*

You're about 30 floors from the ground level. People are shouting at each other to move faster. Others are praying out loud.

Voices are coming through the radio, but it's jumbled and crackled. You can't tell what they're saying. You're almost ready to toss the radio aside.

A firefighter's gear can weigh up to 75 pounds (34 kilograms).

You're exhausted from the weight of everything you're carrying. Your legs are feeling weak.

"We should ditch our gear," Kurt says. "It'll just slow us down if we need to make a run for it."

To dump your air tank and drop your Halligan, turn to page 98.

To keep moving and hold onto your gear, turn to page 100.

Kurt's right. There's no reason to hang onto your air tank and tools. You never made it to the fire anyway.

You unbuckle your pack from your back and let it drop to the floor with the heavy Halligan. You've just lost about 75 pounds of gear. You're still exhausted. But now it'll be easier to move.

A Halligan fire fighting tool

You get close to the third floor when you feel the stairs shake violently. At first you think it's an earthquake, but you know better. You can hear the sound of metal and concrete ripping apart. You look up the stairwell to see the North Tower is collapsing above you. You close your eyes and steel yourself for its crushing weight.

A few moments later, it's completely silent. You can't move, and it's completely dark. When you open your mouth, you taste dust and gravel. Somehow, you're still alive. But the pain is beyond belief. You wait for someone to dig you out before you die from your injuries.

Unfortunately, when they find your lifeless body hours later, it's too late.

THE END

To follow another path, turn to page 9.
To learn more about the events of September 11, 2001, turn to page 103.

As much as you want to ditch your excess weight, you don't want to stop. It doesn't seem possible that both of the Twin Towers could collapse. But you'd rather be safe than sorry.

"Forget it, Kurt," you say. "There's no time. Just keep moving, man."

After what seems like forever, you hit the ground floor. You and Kurt are helping people to the exits when you hear an ominous sound. It sounds like the entire world is shaking. You quickly realize what it is—the North Tower is coming down!

You and Kurt run outside with the rest of the survivors. But you're not safe yet. You keep running as debris falls all around you. Soon, your exhausted legs give out and you fall. Within seconds, you're buried beneath rubble from the North Tower.

You wake up to find yourself in a small pocket of debris. You feel broken and bruised, but you're alive. You use your tools to open a small hole to the surface. You find your radio and call in for help. Finally, a gloved hand reaches in to grab yours.

"Come on out, hero," a guy from another station says. "We've got you."

You emerge from the debris battered and broken, but alive. You're carried to an ambulance where a familiar, dusty face smiles at you from a stretcher. It's Kurt.

"Told you this was our lucky day," he says, coughing.

You're happy you and your partner survived. But today was anything but lucky.

THE END

To follow another path, turn to page 9.
To learn more about the events of September 11, 2001, turn to page 103.

CHAPTER 5

A DAY AMERICA WILL NEVER FORGET

The terrorist attacks in New York City on September 11, 2001, will never be forgotten. The attacks were planned and carried out by a terrorist group called Al-Qaeda. Its leader was Osama Bin Laden. Al-Qaeda had declared a jihad, or a fight against Islam's enemies, against the United States. They believed the U.S. was unjust and were angry at the United States' support of Israel.

The Al-Qaeda terrorists were known to be hiding in Afghanistan. The United States soon went to war in Afghanistan to destroy the terrorist group. Osama Bin Laden was eventually found and killed by a team of U.S. Navy Seals on May 2, 2011.

Close to 3,000 people died during the terrorist attacks on 9/11. Of those killed, 343 were firefighters who died in the line of duty.

The site of the World Trade Center has since been cleared of the rubble. In the footprint of both buildings, large memorial fountains were built. The water pours into a square, the exact shape and dimension of the North and South Towers.

A view of the 9/11 Memorial in New York City

Surrounding the fountains are the names of the people who died during the attacks on New York City. A memorial museum was built between the two fountains to honor those who were lost and to educate the world about what happened on September 11, 2001.

In the years after the attacks, a new World Trade Center building was designed and built. Construction of World Trade Center 1, or Freedom Tower, began on April 27, 2006. The building officially opened on November 3, 2014. Towering above the site of the Twin Towers, Freedom Tower is the tallest building in New York City. It serves as a sign of resistance against terrorism.

MORE TRAGEDY ON 9/11

New York City wasn't the only place struck on September 11. Terrorists also hijacked two other passenger planes. They crashed Flight 77 into the Pentagon in Washington, D.C. This five-sided building serves as the headquarters for the U.S. Department of Defense.

The plane destroyed a large section of the Pentagon's outer ring. The attack killed 59 passengers and crew on Flight 77, 125 people inside the Pentagon, and the five hijackers.

Rubble at the Pentagon on 9/11

It's thought that the terrorists wanted to fly the fourth plane, Flight 93, to Washington, D.C., and crash it into the U.S. Capitol building or the White House.

But passengers on the plane bravely fought the terrorists to stop their plans. Flight 93 never reached the nation's capital. It crashed in an open field near Shanksville, Pennsylvania. All 44 people on board the plane were killed instantly.

9/11 Timeline

7:59 a.m. – American Airlines Flight 11 takes off from Boston, Massachusetts, destined for Los Angeles

8:15 a.m. – United Airlines Flight 175 takes off from Boston, Massachusetts, destined for Los Angeles

8:20 a.m. – American Airlines Flight 77 takes off from Washington, D.C., destined for Los Angeles

8:42 a.m. – United Airlines Flight 93 takes off from Newark, New Jersey, destined for San Francisco

8:46 a.m. – Flight 11 crashes into North Tower of World Trade Center

9:03 a.m. – Flight 175 crashes into South Tower of World Trade Center

9:37 a.m. – Flight 77 crashes into the Pentagon

9:59 a.m. – World Trade Center South Tower collapses

10:03 a.m. – Flight 93 crashes near Shanksville, Pennsylvania, after passengers storm the cockpit

10:15 a.m. – Collapse of Pentagon E Ring

10:28 a.m. – World Trade Center North Tower collapses

12:16 p.m. – U.S. airspace closed to all air traffic

12:30 p.m. – 14 survivors found in ruins of North Tower's Stairwell B

5:20 p.m. – Building 7 of World Trade Center collapses

8:30 p.m. – President George W. Bush addresses the nation

Other Paths to Explore

1. Imagine that you were one of the passengers on Flight 93. The plane has been hijacked by terrorists, and you're not sure what's going to happen. Would you try to resist the terrorists? What could you do to survive? Would you be willing to risk your life to save yourself and the rest of the passengers?

2. Think about what it was like to work in the Pentagon on the morning of 9/11. You've watched the news reports of the two planes crashing into the World Trade Center. Then, a short time later, another plane slams into the side of your building. How would you respond? Would you run for safety? Would you stay and help look for survivors? How could you assist the first responders who are racing to the scene?

3. Imagine you live in Lower Manhattan in New York City. From your apartment, you saw both planes crash into the World Trade Center. What would you do? Would you be afraid to leave your home? Would you try to help people running through the streets? How might your life change after seeing the destruction of your neighborhood?

Select Bibliography

9/11 Memorial: September 11 Attack Timeline. https://timeline.911memorial.org/#Timeline/2/AudioEntry/12

"9/11 Timeline: Three Hours That Changed Everything," by Nick Routley, Visual Capitalist, September 8, 2021, https://www.visualcapitalist.com/9-11-timeline-three-hours-that-changed-everything/

"The Attack on the Pentagon," Naval History and Heritage Command Archives, https://www.history.navy.mil/research/archives/digital-exhibits-highlights/photo-galleries-9-11/pentagon-attack.html

"I Escaped From the 80th Floor of the North Tower on 9/11 – Then it Collapsed on Me," by Sharon Premoli, Independent, September 11, 2021, https://www.independent.co.uk/news/world/americas/september-11-anniversary-survivor-story-b1917176.html

The National 9/11 Pentagon Memorial, U.S. Department of Defense. https://www.defense.gov/Multimedia/Experience/Pentagon-Memorial/

"September 11 Attacks," by Peter L. Bergen, Encyclopedia Britannica, https://www.britannica.com/event/September-11-attacks

Terrorism Timeline, Since 9/11. https://since911.com/explore/terrorism-timeline#jump_time_item_393

"What Was Flight 93's Target?" by Farrell Evans, History.com, August 19, 2021, https://www.history.com/news/flight-93-target-september-11

Glossary

cancer (KAN-suhr)—a disease in which abnormal cells grow faster than normal and destroy healthy organs and tissues in a person's body

chaotic (kay-AH-tik)—totally confused and disorganized

disintegrate (dis-IN-tuh-grayt)—to break apart or blow up into small pieces

FDNY (eff-DEE-en-why)—short for the Fire Department of the City of New York

Halligan (HAL-uh-guhn)—a heavy metal tool used by firefighters to pry open doors or break through walls in rescue efforts

iconic (eye-KAH-nuhk)—an object or person that is considered especially important or impressive or stands as a symbol for something

Mayday (MAY-day)—a distress call in radio communications, used to alert people of something dangerous happening

paramedic (pair-uh-MEH-dik)—a medical worker who often travels in an ambulance to treat hurt or sick people in emergency situations

relay (REE-lay)—a system of gear or equipment that is connected together to accomplish a task

SCBA (ESS-see-bee-ay)—short for Self-Contained Breathing Apparatus; a system that includes an air tank, a mask, and a breathing regulator

terrorist (TER-uhr-ist)—someone who uses violence and threats to create fear and achieve their extreme political or religious goals

Read More

Maranville, Amy. *The 9/11 Terrorist Attacks: A Day That Changed America*. North Mankato, MN: Capstone, 2022.

Romero, Libby. *September 11*. Washington, D.C.: National Geographic, 2021.

Rusick, Jessica. *Ground Zero: Then and Now*. North Mankato, MN: ABDO and Daughters, 2021.

Internet Sites

9/11 Memorial: September 11 Attack Timeline
timeline.911memorial.org/#Timeline/2

Remembering September 11
kids.nationalgeographic.com/history/article/remembering-september-11

September 11 Facts for Kids
kids.kiddle.co/September_11_attacks

JOIN OTHER HISTORICAL ADVENTURES WITH MORE
YOU CHOOSE SEEKING HISTORY!

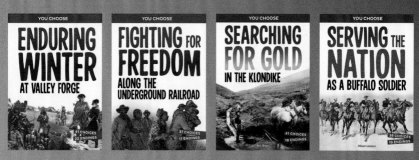

About the Author

Thomas Kingsley Troupe is the author of more than 200 books for young readers. He's written books about everything from 3rd grade werewolves to talking spaceships, and everything paranormal and creepy you can think of. He wrote his first book when he was in 2nd grade and has been making up stories ever since. Thomas was a firefighter/EMT for 13 years, serving the city of Woodbury, Minnesota, where he lives with his two sons.